LITTLE FOX CAN I WAIT TO DREAM

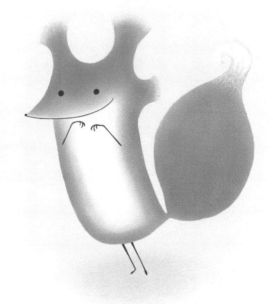

Rhea Pechter

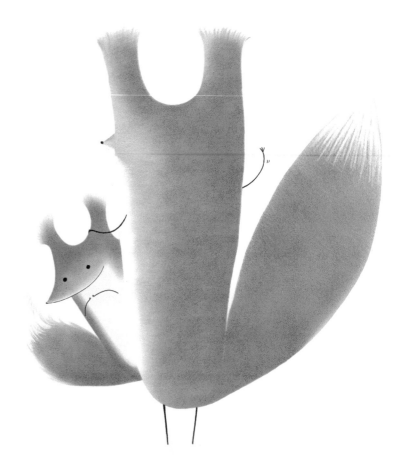

Typesetting and design by Peter Kaloroumakis

Library of Congress Control Number: 2018910667

Paperback ISBN: 978-1-7327459-0-2

For the tiny people, who have listened so well.

♥Leo♥Zach♥Ruby♥Benjamin♥
♥Nicholas♥Nathaniel♥Matthew♥Andrew♥Reese♥
Violet♥Kingston♥Atticus♥EzeKiel♥Addie♥Oskar♥Max♥
Britton♥Charlize♥Lea♥Logan♥Madeline♥Grayson♥Rosie♥Callie
Simon♥Lucas♥Enzo♥Hattie♥Evan♥Vera♥Ari♥Macy♥Spencer♥Ella
Laurel♥LiLi♥Gracie♥Callum♥Theo♥Jayden♥Jaxen♥Trey♥Ellie♥Luke♥Marin♥Xo
Jonas♥Hank♥Avery♥Pete♥Eli♥Jaxon♥Ava♥Elijah♥Noah♥Malcolm♥Lincoln♥Elliott
Sophie♥Wesley♥Penelope♥Chryssa♥London♥Silas♥Willow♥Karin♥Bryce♥Zoe♥Alba♥Tom
MiKaela♥Hailee♥Chase♥Journey♥Ornella♥Dean♥Emma♥Magnus♥Pia♥Jason♥Just Kai♥
Liliana♥Sofia♥Emilia♥Olivia♥Jude♥Beau♥Marisol♥Megan♥Carsten♥Oliver♥Hadlee♥
Sawyer♥Maddie Lynn♥Madison♥Kacandra♥Izzy♥Gertie♥Vivian♥Jac♥Jessa♥Lily♥Ben♥
Kate♥Juniper♥Caroline♥Heidi♥Kieran♥Otto♥Lucia♥Clara♥Felix♥Bailey♥Keira♥Matty♥Mira♥
Julian♥Michael♥John-Patrick♥Declan♥Nunu♥Avi♥NiK♥Flannery♥Phoebe♥Junia♥Riley♥
Young♥Dayden♥Dottie♥Ida♥Ros♥Gemma♥Connor♥Margaret♥Marie♥Bella♥India♥
Mei♥Jubilee♥Josie♥Mustafa♥Sophia♥Dennis♥Celeste♥Marion♥April♥Matt♥Peter♥Thomas♥
Alexandra♥Vasiliki♥Alaina♥Sarah♥Isaac♥Ella♥Atlin♥Case♥Indie♥Brennan♥Weston♥
Nathan♥Isaiah♥Lydia♥William♥Olukai♥Ayodele♥Ailey♥Fiona♥Eleanor♥HB3♥
Annabelle♥Bayley♥Claire♥Tara♥Sybil♥Evie♥Becca♥Taryn♥Paisley♥Isabella♥
Rena♥Nora♥Sam♥Colette♥Simone♥Ayla♥Jasper♥Oliver♥Roland♥Elaina♥
Troy♥Jack♥Cecilia♥Lana♥An Binh♥Grace♥Miriam♥Sivan♥Elise♥Norah♥
Ferrán♥Salma♥Javi♥Aida♥Walter♥Ece♥Taira♥Liam♥Noa♥Pascale♥
Evryn♥Serena♥Brianna♥Ellis♥Hugh♥Gabriel♥Angelo♥Huxley♥Kaiella♥
Freddy♥Wolfie♥Emilyn♥Lane♥Olive♥Amelia♥Alaina♥Ana Sofia♥
Alexis♥Kaley♥Hugo♥Theadora♥Quinn♥Neil♥Katie♥Arthur♥Kendall♥
Franklin♥Catherine♥Ethan♥Anjali♥Amar♥Asha♥Drew♥Charli♥Santino♥
Valentina♥Roop♥Noor♥Caleb♥Lily♥James♥Nora♥Eden♥Margo♥Clem♥
Griffin♥Ivy♥Emmett♥Izzy Mae♥Gus♥Olin♥Maxwell♥Joey♥Mary♥
Benny♥Hailey♥Tristan♥Ellison♥Parker♥Addison♥Zara♥Chloe♥Emily♥
Clea♥Brinkley♥Cora♥Julia♥Lauren♥Kennedy♥Charlotte♥Scarlett♥
Memphis♥Lawson♥Judson♥Timothy♥Avery♥Natalie♥Caden♥Brayden♥Sy
Ella Kate♥Annie♥Henry♥Charlie♥Layla♥Wyatt♥Jayce♥Jaden♥
Frankie♥Irene♥Isaac♥Owen♥Dylan♥Madelyn♥
Indigo♥Joselyn♥James♥Nicky♥
Lakshya♥Lia

♥Dante♥Gloria♥Cliff♥Maya♥
Danny♥Audrey♥Paul♥Kathryn♥Corinne♥Gianna♥
Ellia♥Cade♥Beckett♥Vivienne♥Estela♥Pem♥Beth♥Tyler♥
Xander♥Satya♥Brandon♥Sydney Lou♥Lenci♥Naeem♥Nia♥
Alina♥Suhana♥Rehan♥Annabel♥Rowan♥Daphne♥Pierce♥Molly♥Pax
Hannah♥Nayomi♥Natasa♥Sabina♥Nic♥Savannah♥Beatrice♥Riley♥Ezra
Kelsey♥Maximus♥Eloise♥Aleena♥Saydee♥Sage♥Zachariah♥Tia
Abigail♥Candace♥Dexter♥Millie♥Sarina♥Claudia♥Eryn♥Vikram♥
Ursa♥John♥Evelyn♥June♥Isla♥Arlo♥Nikhil♥Akira♥Sakura♥Amber♥Ed
August♥Azalea♥Baylor♥Cole♥Emilie♥Connie♥David♥Juliet♥Ember♥Emma♥Elsa
Finley♥Gavin♥Harrison♥Ibrahim♥Isobel♥Jillian♥Jonathan♥Josh♥Lucille♥Ty
Lucy♥Luella♥Minoux♥Piper♥Margot♥Marina♥Maryam♥Mason♥Nolan
Pippa♥Ryan♥Sadhana♥Samantha♥Sangam♥Seamus♥Teagan♥Toff♥Wally♥Briella
Tessa♥Amaris♥Ishani♥Lilly♥Liz♥Maple♥Mila♥Payton♥Rosa♥Stella♥Israel
Barrett♥Joseph♥Constantine♥Geraldine♥Victoria♥Terrence♥Stephan♥Howard
Clementine♥Bernard♥Clarence♥Henley♥Frederick♥Tatiana♥Carter♥Carson♥Bo
Cleo♥Bennett♥Odie♥Sela♥Mia♥Shepherd♥Perry♥Alexander♥Harper♥Maria
Amaya♥Kylie♥Ali♥Austin♥Lailah♥Nahla♥Scott♥Pierre♥Jackson♥
Emory♥Amali♥Lena♥Perry♥Sabrina♥Natalia♥Andre♥Asher
Sandra♥George♥Adrian♥Taylor♥Valencia♥Alexi♥Kendi♥Eva♥Issa♥Li
Aida♥Helen♥Gloria♥Annika♥Isabel♥Ely♥Josh♥Jasmine♥Rachel
Cierra♥Joel♥Maryam♥Gwendolyn♥Raphael♥Georgiana♥Kendrick
Natasha♥Zack♥Christopher♥Wells♥Emerson♥Meg♥Lark♥Mateo
Marco♥Belle♥Darrell♥Devin♥Iris♥Noam♥Curtis♥Maddox♥
Maia♥Reid♥Nolyn♥Miles♥Blair♥Ian♥Amelie
Grady♥Kara♥Rosalie♥Nicole♥Eugenie♥
Clyde♥Tara♥Aria♥Elias♥Rebecca♥
Sebastian♥Mila♥Ollie♥
Landon♥Hunter♥Lo

As soon as Auntie was out of sight,

Little Fox slipped away, her pawsteps light.

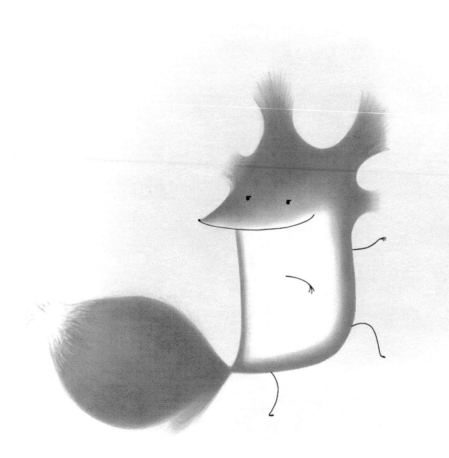

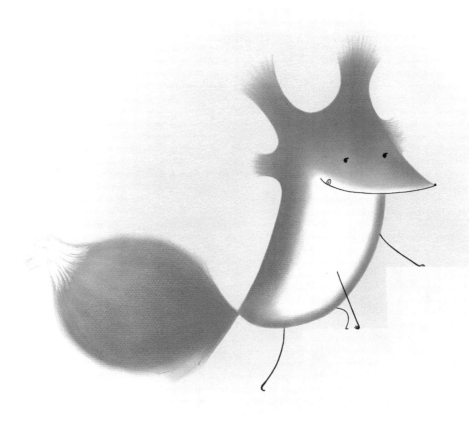

The only sound as she climbed each stair

was the soft *swish swish* of her tail through the air.

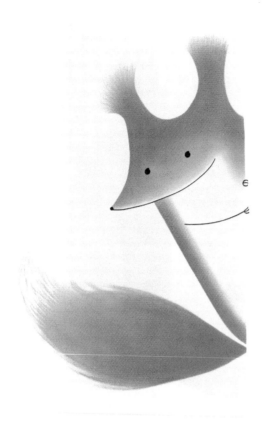

Climbing into bed Little Fox was elated.

Finally her thirst for new dreams would be sated.

She pulled up her covers, closed her eyes with a grin,

and waited for the night's dreams to begin.

Little Fox slowed her breath and hugged her tail to her heart...

Then Auntie yelled

"Little Fox!"

and she sat up with a start.

Little Fox sighed as Auntie came near.

"It's not bedtime yet," Auntie said.

"What are you doing in here?"

"Auntie, I have so many dreams to get to tonight.

Now, when you leave, can you turn out the light?"

"I see," Auntie said.

"That *is* a good reason to sneak off to bed.

But change your clothes first, little niece.

Come now, which PJs? Flannel or fleece?"

Little Fox shrugged. "Fleece, I guess."

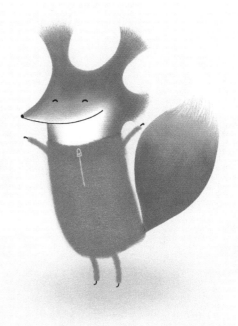

And lickety-split she was suitably dressed.

Little Fox clambered into her bed.

"I'm ready to dream, Auntie. I have such a long night ahead.

A bevy of dreams is now on its way.

Soon I'll float down a river on a warm summer day,

on a raft made of watermelons that double as treats.

I'll spit the seeds up to birds; they'll rejoin me with tweets!"

"Sounds like quite an adventure to have in your sleep,

but let's brush your teeth before you count any sheep."

Little Fox sighed as she headed for the sink.

She polished every tooth, quick as a wink.

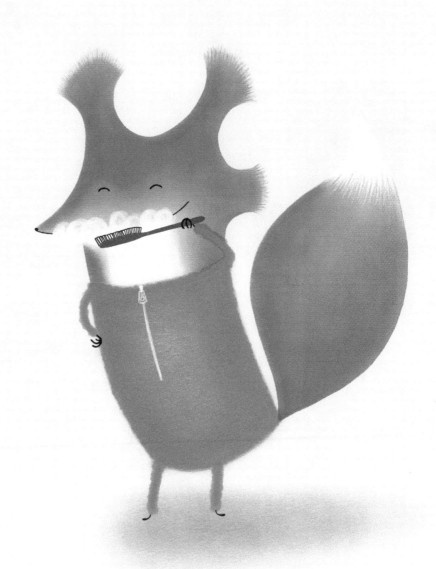

With her teeth sparkling, Little Fox climbed into bed.

"I'm ready to dream, Auntie. I have such a long night ahead.

Soon I'll be hitching a ride through a garden in spring

holding ever so tight to a honeybee's wing

as he dips and dives, pollinating flowers.

Oh Auntie, I think I could do that for hours."

"Look," Auntie said, "I'd love to see my way out,
but I can't let you snooze with your toys strewn about."

"Very well," Little Fox said as she picked up a train.
"I prefer a clean room, Auntie, no need to explain."

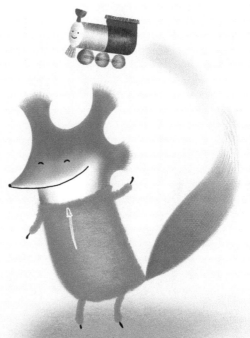

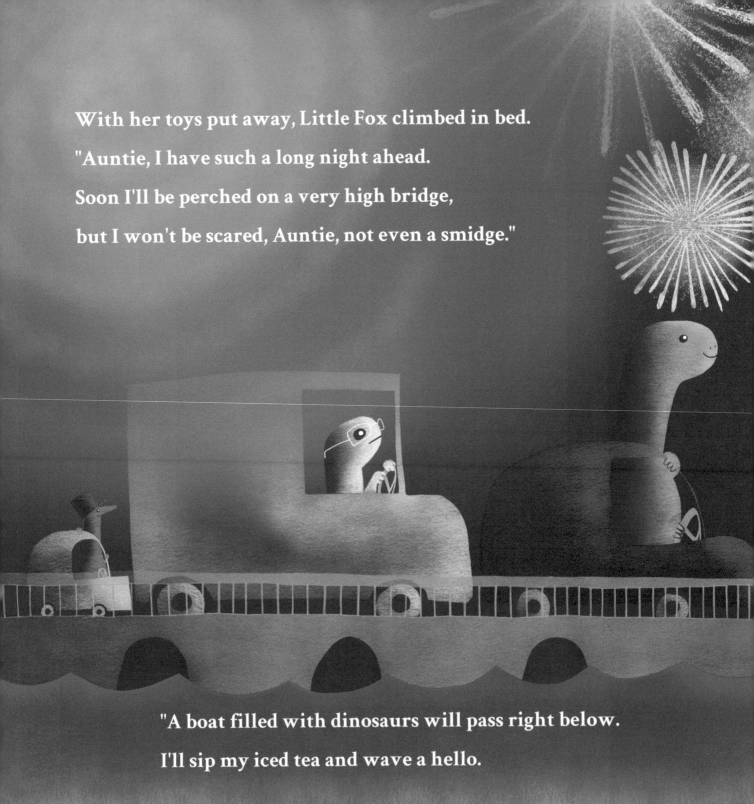

With her toys put away, Little Fox climbed in bed.

"Auntie, I have such a long night ahead.

Soon I'll be perched on a very high bridge,

but I won't be scared, Auntie, not even a smidge."

"A boat filled with dinosaurs will pass right below.

I'll sip my iced tea and wave a hello.

As their celebration sails on by,
they'll set off fireworks that'll paint the sky."

Little Fox pulled her blanket up to her chin.

"Now, Auntie? Is it time to turn in?"

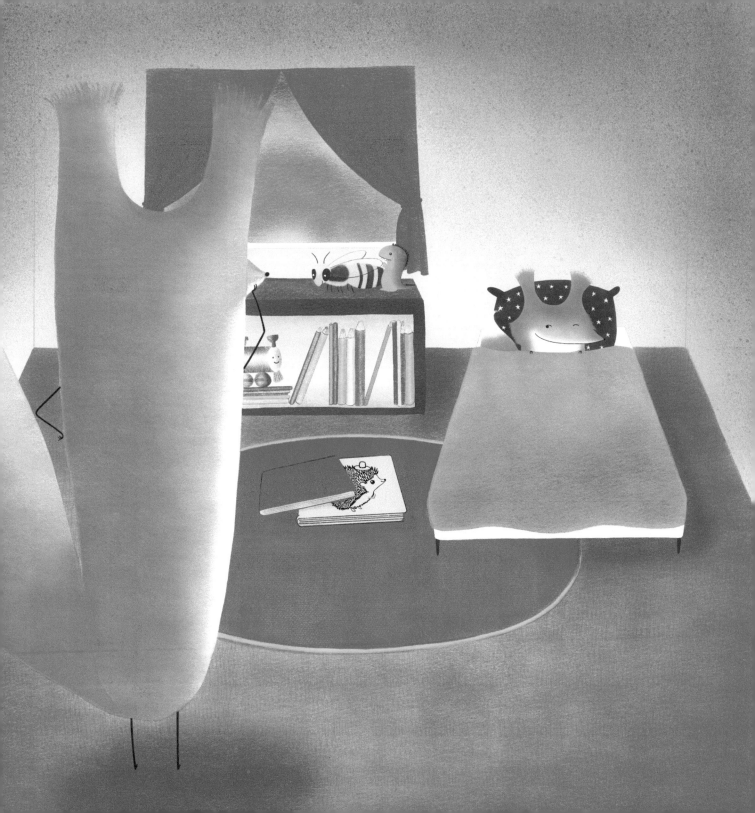

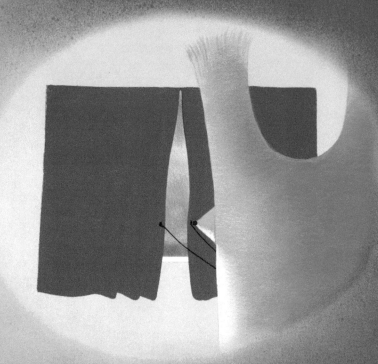

Auntie drew the drapes and returned some books to the shelf.

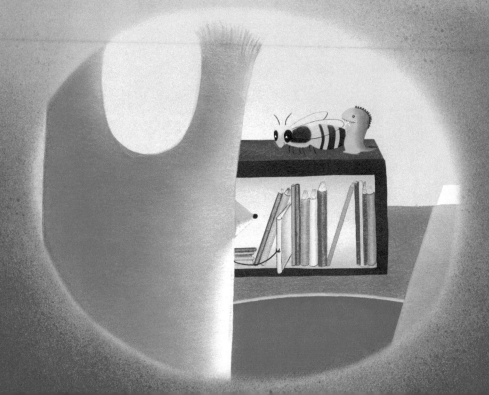

"You win this time, my little elf.

Your toys are stored, your teeth are bright.

You are properly dressed for the night.

It *is* still early, but I admire your scheming,

so ..."Auntie glanced back—

Little Fox was already dreaming.

Auntie kissed Little Fox's paw and whispered goodnight...

and when she left,

she turned out the light.

CPSIA information can be obtained
at www.ICGtesting.com
Printed in the USA
LVHW071931300720
661976LV00002B/30